MAGNETS
Inquiry Investigations
Questioning, Exploration, and Discovery

by Barbara J. Fagenbaum

Carson-Dellosa Publishing Company

Greensboro, NC

Credits

Editor: Erin Seltzer

Layout Design: Mark Conrad

Inside Illustrations: Christopher P. Pappas

Cover Design: Matthew Van Zomeren

Cover Photos: Matthew Van Zomeren

©2004, Carson-Dellosa Publishing Company, Inc., Greensboro, North Carolina 27425. The purchase of this material entitles the buyer to reproduce worksheets and activities for classroom use only—not for commercial resale. Reproduction of these materials for an entire school or district is prohibited. No part of this book may be reproduced (except as noted above), stored in a retrieval system, or transmitted in any form or by any means (mechanically, electronically, recording, etc.) without the prior written consent of Carson-Dellosa Publishing Co., Inc.

Printed in the USA • All rights reserved.

ISBN 0-88724-265-0

Table of Contents

Introduction 4
   What is inquiry-based learning? 4
   How do I use *Inquiry Investigations: Magnets* in my classroom? 4
   How is each investigation organized? 5

Magnet Safety and Storage 6

Literature Connections 7

Individual Assessment 8

Inquiry Investigations Lessons 9
   Investigation 1: What are magnets? 9
   Investigation 1: reproducible for Home Investigation 10
   Investigation 2: How can magnets help me find hidden objects? 11
   Investigation 3: What materials are attracted to magnets? 13
   Investigation 4: What metals are attracted to magnets? 14
   Investigation 4: reproducible for Home Investigation 15
   Investigation 5: How can iron be separated from cereal? 16
   Investigation 6: Do magnets only attract? 18
   Investigation 7: What is special about the ends of bar magnets? 19
   Investigation 8: What is a magnetic field? 20
   Investigation 9: Can magnetism travel through other objects? 22
   Investigation 9: reproducible for Home Investigation 24
   Investigation 10: How strong is my magnet? 25
   Investigation 11: How can I make my own magnet? 26
   Investigation 12: How can I demagnetize a magnet? 28
   Investigation 13: What is an electromagnet? 29
   Investigation 14: How does electromagnetic strength change? 30
   Investigation 15: How can I use magnets for fun? 31
   Investigation 15: reproducible for Home Investigation.............................. 32

Discovery Journal J1
   Reproducibles for Investigations 1-15 .... J1-J16

Introduction

Inquiry Investigations: Magnets offers interesting and motivating inquiry-based activities that help each student build a foundational understanding of magnetism. Each investigation begins with a question. Through hands-on activities, brainstorming, discussion, sharing, and demonstration, students answer the opening question and other questions that they ask along the way. The study of magnets concludes with Magnet Fun Day. Here, students create and present activities that use magnets.

What is inquiry-based learning?

Inquiry-based learning is an instructional approach that encourages students to actively think rather than passively absorb information. Students are presented with questions or problems and are given materials to manipulate, experiment with, and explore. This guided exploration leads to further questioning and discovery. Inquiry-based learning results in an enduring understanding of each concept.

An inquiry approach to scientific discovery is a systematic approach that incorporates a wide variety of activities. Students, like scientists, engage in research, observation, questioning, planning investigations, experimenting, analyzing data, and proposing answers. Demonstrations can be used to motivate interest, to strengthen process skills, and to present information on particular concepts. Hands-on activities give students opportunities to utilize and develop science process skills. Guided questions help students think like scientists by leading students to evaluate information and pose more questions. These activities encourage inquiry, which helps lead to the goal of discovery. You will be a facilitator in this process.

An important part of inquiry-based learning is the time students spend seeking answers to their own questions. Whenever possible, particularly when students are highly motivated and actively engaged, give them extra time to direct their own learning. This type of extended activity may seem like play to your students, but deep learning will occur. You may need to modify the lessons and/or journal questions to incorporate your students' new discoveries.

How do I use *Inquiry Investigations: Magnets* in my classroom?

This book is divided into two sections: teacher pages and reproducible student Discovery Journal pages. The **Inquiry Investigation Lessons** are your guides for the investigations. Read them in advance, gather materials, and make necessary preparations. The **Discovery Journal** pages guide and enhance each student's investigation experience. Have students use construction paper for the covers of their Discovery Journals. Copy and staple together one set of journal pages for each student so that the journals can be used with each investigation. Each Discovery Journal provides directions for the student, places to record observations, and questions that lead to deeper thinking.

Begin your study of magnets by providing quality literature about magnets for your class. This literacy integration provides resource materials for further exploration and gives students opportunities to develop their expository reading skills. Use the recommendations from the **Literature Connections** section (page 7) to start your collection and add students' selections.

The **Individual Assessment** section (page 8) provides a convenient record keeping tool. The sheet can be used to assess general science skills and how students use their Discovery Journals. It also provides an area for comments. A completed assessment can become part of a student's file, portfolio, or report card.

Introduction

Next, have a brainstorming session to activate prior knowledge and assess what students already know about magnets. Label chart paper with "What I Know About Magnets." Label another piece "What I Wonder About Magnets." List everything students tell you about magnets even if their responses are scientifically incorrect. These misconceptions and inaccuracies will be addressed during the investigations. Some students may correct the errors of others. Turn these differences into questions and record them on the "What I Wonder About Magnets" chart. Record other questions on this chart, as well. Although the investigations in this book build on each other, students do not have to complete every investigation or begin with the first investigation in this book.

How is each investigation organized?

Each investigation begins with a question. The primary concept that students should learn from the investigation is found in the Enduring Knowledge section. In inquiry-based learning, there is no single objective for each lesson. Rather, a primary concept develops into foundational knowledge. Many students will learn more than just the primary concept. An investigation can last for one day or longer depending upon your students' interests, abilities, and knowledge. Students can extend that knowledge by seeking answers to their own questions. (They can continue exploring a concept in a science center, for example.) Encourage this student-led learning as much as possible.

The science process skills used (observing, measuring, communicating, classifying, inferring, and predicting,) are listed for each investigation. When students **observe**, they use all of the senses to notice characteristics, responses, changes, and behaviors. Accurate **measurements** help ensure conclusions based on observations and experiences. Students **communicate** their ideas and questions throughout each investigation.

Students also **classify**, or group, similar objects, patterns, or behaviors together; this process helps students connect new knowledge to prior knowledge. Although making **inferences** can be challenging, students' inferences become the basis for **predictions** and further exploration.

Fast Facts are given to add interest and motivation. This information can be shared with students at any time. Each investigation lists vocabulary words that students might not understand. Use these terms regularly throughout the investigations and periodically review their meanings with students.

Introduce students to the concept posed in the question by following the guidelines in the Getting Ready section. Facilitate the investigation with the help of the Guided Exploration section. Students are often asked to work in small groups. These groups usually work best if there are no more than four students in each. Throughout this time, encourage students to explore. Ask open-ended questions to enhance discovery. Question starters include, "How else can you…? What would happen if you…? What else could you do to…?"

The Reflection and Analysis section has guiding questions to encourage students to think beyond the basics. Analysis and evaluation are important components of inquiry and lead students to deeper levels of understanding. Some investigations include a Home Investigation activity to extend students' exploration.

Time spent on *Inquiry Investigations* is time spent in exploration and discovery. This approach is an active learning experience for students. Students will move around the classroom, share ideas, discuss problems, seek answers, and form new questions. Learn with them!

Magnet Safety and Storage

Magnets can permanently damage some items.

Do not use magnets near:
- computers
- computer equipment
- CD or tape players
- digital cameras
- electronic equipment
- CD-ROMs
- videotapes
- audiotapes
- watches
- credit cards

- Exposure to heat and harsh contact with the floor or other objects can decrease a magnet's strength.
- Store magnets away from heat.
- Avoid dropping magnets.

- Properly stored magnets will last a long time.
- Keep magnets in containers with lids.
- If you store many magnets in one container, place them side by side with opposite poles together. For horseshoe magnets, place plates or rods of soft iron on the ends to connect the magnets' poles.

Literature Connections

When teaching about magnets, the following books make great additions to your classroom library. The books can be resources for sparking curiosity and questions. Selections can be read aloud in part or in full, depending upon the investigations and interests of your students. The books by Don Wulffson and Charlotte Jones (*) will be especially helpful for students while working on Investigation 15 (page 31).

Amazing Magnetism by Rebecca Carmi (Scholastic, 2002).

Electricity and Magnetism by Terry Jennings (Steck-Vaughn, 1996).

Jake Drake, Know-It-All #2 by Andrew Clements (Simon & Schuster Children's, 2001).

**The Kid Who Invented the Popsicle: And Other Surprising Stories About Inventions* by Don L. Wulffson (Puffin, 1999).

Magnetism by John Hudson Tiner (Smart Apple Media, 2002).

Magnets by Karen Bryant-Mole (Heinemann Library, 2002).

Magnets by Jason Cooper (The Rourke Book Company, Inc., 2003).

Magnets by Darlene Lauw and Lim Cheng Puay (Crabtree, 2001).

Magnets by Steve Parker (Gareth Stevens, 1998).

Magnets by Ann Schreiber (Grosset & Dunlap, 2003).

Magnets: Pulling Together, Pushing Apart by Natalie M. Rosinsky (Picture Window Books, 2002).

Mickey's Magnet by Franklyn M. Branley and Eleanor K. Vaughan (Scholastic, 1976).

**Mistakes That Worked* by Charlotte Jones (Doubleday Books for Young Readers, 1994).

Science Magic with Magnets by Chris Oxlade (Barron's Educational Series, 1995).

The Usborne Book of Batteries and Magnets (How to Make Series) by Paula Borton and Vicky Cave (EDC Publications, 1995).

What Makes a Magnet? by Franklyn M. Branley (HarperTrophy, 1996).

Individual Assessment
Inquiry Investigations: Magnets

Student Name: _____
Date: _____

Key
3 = exceeds expectations
2 = independently meets expectations
1 = needs support to meet expectations

Investigations
_____ follows safety rules
_____ works respectfully with peers
_____ follows directions
_____ participates in discussions
_____ uses materials appropriately
_____ makes thoughtful predictions
_____ makes accurate observations
_____ draws reasonable conclusions
_____ poses thoughtful questions for further inquiry

Discovery Journal
_____ follows procedures for investigations
_____ clearly records data
_____ completes illustrations with care and accuracy
_____ clearly states reasoning for conclusions

Observation Notes
_____
_____
_____
_____
_____
_____
_____
_____
_____
_____
_____

Investigation 1

What are magnets?

Enduring Knowledge
Magnets are pieces of metal that pull or attract other pieces of metal.

Process Skills
communicating, inferring, observing, predicting

Fast Facts
Magnets come in a variety of shapes: bars, thick discs, and squares. A horseshoe magnet is a bar magnet in the shape of a U.

Vocabulary
attract, magnet, metal

Getting Ready
Gather students for a group discussion. Pose the question, "What do you know about magnets?" Have students record information in their Discovery Journals. Record some responses on the board, chart paper, or overhead transparency. Explain that students will work in groups to find an answer to the question "What is a magnet?" Ask students to share how they might test an idea that was listed in their responses. Model one or two student responses to show how to test a magnet. If desired, have each student place his Discovery Journal on a clipboard to make recording observations easier.

Materials for Each Student
- clipboard (optional)
- Discovery Journal
- magnet
- pencil

Guided Exploration
Give each student a magnet to test objects at her desk and around the classroom. Before students move around the room, have them describe their magnets in their Discovery Journals. Tell students that these descriptions will be used to create lists of characteristics or properties they discover about their magnets.

Reflection and Analysis
After students have completed exploration time, group them into teams of four. In their teams, have each student share one thing he discovered about his magnet. Give the teams time to try their team members' discoveries. Then, have students work together to answer question 7 (page J1) in their Discovery Journals. Have a member from each team share the team's definition with the class. Then, discuss the following questions as a class.

Guiding Questions:
- What do the things that were attracted to your magnets have in common?
- What do the things that were not attracted to your magnets have in common?
- How could you further test your definition of a magnet?

Home Investigation
The Home Investigation on page 10 gives students opportunities to find science in their daily home lives. Have students look for magnets in their homes and record how they use the magnets.

Home Investigation

Name: _____ Date: _____

Investigation 1: What is a magnet?

Search your home for magnets. Look in the kitchen, the garage, the living room, and other places. Ask your family members to help you. In the chart below, write where you found each magnet and how it is used.

Where I Found the Magnet	How It Is Used
1.	
2.	
3.	
4.	
5.	

How are magnets useful?

_____
_____
_____
_____
_____
_____
_____
_____

Investigation 2

How can magnets help me find hidden objects?

Enduring Knowledge
Magnets can explore areas not visible to people.

Process Skills
communicating, inferring, observing

Fast Facts
A medical diagnostic tool called Magnetic Resonance Imaging (MRI) uses a magnetic field and radio waves to produce images of the patient's internal body parts.

Vocabulary
grid, visible

Materials for Getting Ready
- 10 boxes with lids (shoe boxes, gift boxes)
- 10 copies of grid pattern (page 12)
- 10 metal items attracted by magnets (scissors, paper clip, nail, stapler, ruler, barrette, screwdriver, jar lid, etc.)
- glue

Getting Ready
Use boxes with lids to set up 10 different stations around the classroom. For each station, reproduce the grid pattern (page 12) and glue a grid onto the top of each box. Gather ten items that are attracted to magnets. Securely tape one item under the top of each lid. If possible, place the item in the center of a grid square. Place the lid on the box and label the box with a station number.

Share with students that objects are located in boxes around the room. Explain that students will only use magnets to find each item's location in its box.

Ask students to brainstorm how to use magnets to find the missing objects. After they share and show ideas for using magnets, model sliding a magnet over the top of a box without lifting or shaking the magnet. After finding the object, model how students should record the item's location in their Discovery Journals. Some items, such as scissors, will cover more than one square on the grid. Clarify what students should do in this situation. Tell students how you will signal to move to the next station.

Materials for Each Student
- Discovery Journal
- magnet
- pencil

Guided Exploration
Have two or more students visit each station at a time. Allow approximately five minutes at each station for students to use their magnets and record their findings. When the allotted time has passed, have students rotate stations. Circulate among the groups to support and encourage exploration.

Reflection and Analysis
Gather students and reveal the location of each item. Before lifting the lid to identify the item, have students guess what the object is based on how much area or how many squares attracted magnets. After predictions, show the item. Repeat for each box, then use the questions for a class discussion.

Guiding Questions:
- How did a magnet help you?
- If you repeated this investigation, what would you do differently?
- What did you learn about magnets?

© Carson-Dellosa — CD-2362 *Inquiry Investigations: Magnets*

Investigation 2

Grid Pattern

	A	B	C	D
6				
5				
4				
3				
2				
1				

Investigation 3

What materials are attracted to magnets?

Enduring Knowledge
Magnets attract certain types of metals.

Process Skills
classifying, communicating, inferring, observing, predicting

Fast Facts
Magnets are made of steel that has been magnetized with electricity. Some magnets are made of iron or alloys.

Vocabulary
prediction

Materials for Getting Ready
- paper bags
- objects to test for magnetism such as wood blocks, pennies, paper clips, metal and plastic lids, erasers, metal and plastic spoons, marshmallows, tissues, wires, nails, crayons, etc.

Getting Ready
Collect a variety of objects including some items made of different metals. Place six items in each bag and create one bag for each group of students. The contents of the bags do not need to be identical.

Lead a discussion about predicting and guessing. Guide students to understand that a guess is based on little, if any, supporting information, but a prediction is based on experience, knowledge, and supporting evidence. Model an example of predicting if an object will be attracted to a magnet. Hold up an object, such as a stapler, and think aloud to students.

Explain your reasoning for your prediction and ask students to provide more evidence. Pose more questions about how the magnet might interact with the stapler. For example, will the magnet attract all areas of the stapler? What areas might not be attracted to a magnet? Finally, test the predictions with a magnet.

Materials for Each Student
- Discovery Journal
- magnet
- pencil

Guided Exploration
After the discussion, give each group a bag and instruct students to record the name of each item, from what material it is primarily made, and their predictions of magnetic attraction in their Discovery Journals. Explain that after making predictions, students will test their ideas and finish answering the questions (page J3) in their Discovery Journals.

Reflection and Analysis
Conclude this investigation by having students discuss their findings. Use the following questions to help students develop understanding.

Guiding Questions:
- What item surprised you most?
- What items were attracted to the magnet?
- What items were not attracted to the magnet?
- A penny is made of metal. Why do you think the penny was not attracted to the magnet?
- Do we need to change our definition of a magnet? Why or why not?

Investigation 4

What metals are attracted to magnets?

Enduring Knowledge
Magnets attract only some metals, primarily iron and steel.

Process Skills
classifying, communicating, inferring, observing, predicting

Fast Facts
Magnets attract iron and steel as well as nickel and cobalt. Metals not attracted by magnets include aluminum, brass, bronze, copper, gold, silver, stainless steel, and tin. Tin cans are often made of steel with a light coat of tin. Straight pins are made of steel or brass coated with silver. Pennies are made of bronze.

Vocabulary
aluminum, brass, bronze, copper, gold, iron, nickel, silver, stainless steel, steel, tin

Getting Ready
Have students brainstorm different names and kinds of metals. Record their responses on chart paper. Explain that Earth is basically a giant rock made of elements, including many metals. Show examples of various metals and products that use them.

Facts about Metals:
- Metals form a large part of Earth.
- Metals are not often found in pure form but in combination with other materials.
- Iron ore is a common, widely-used metal.
- Iron ore is used to make many types of iron and steel.
- Refining, or purifying, iron ore makes steel.
- People have used gold, silver, copper, and iron for thousands of years.
- Metals are melted under high heat to create desired shapes.

Materials for Each Group
- 1 bag
- collection of metallic items
- Discovery Journals
- magnet for each student
- pencils

Guided Exploration
Prior to the exploration, place objects from the list of metal products (page J5) in a bag for each group of two to four students. Names and metallic content of US coins are listed on the chart. If you know appropriate information, you can use the names and metallic contents of coins from other countries. Give each group a bag of magnetic and non-magnetic metallic items. Have students test the magnetic properties of the items and record their results on page J4 in their Discovery Journals.

Reflection and Analysis
Discuss the guiding questions and have groups write rules about what magnets attract.

Guiding Questions:
- What items were attracted to the magnet? From what metals are they made?
- Which metals were not attracted to the magnet?
- Which objects did you predict would be attracted to the magnet but were not?
- What do you know about the metals used to make those objects that were not attracted to the magnet?

Home Investigation
Students will use magnets to find iron and steel in their homes. Remind students to keep magnets away from computers, videotapes, audiotapes, disks, credit cards, watches, cameras, etc.

Home Investigation

Name: _____ Date: _____

Investigation 4: What metals are attracted to magnets?

Be a metal detector. Search your home for iron and steel. Use a magnet to uncover these hidden materials. Look everywhere. Ask your family to help you. Make a list of the items you found that you think are made of iron or steel.

Do NOT test the magnet on computers or computer items including disks. Do NOT test videotapes or audiotapes. Do NOT test credit-type cards, watches, or any electronic equipment (cameras, CD players, etc.)

Things Made of Iron or Steel

1. Do all metal objects look like they are made of metal? Explain.

_____
_____
_____

2. What would be different in your home if there were no iron or steel?

_____
_____
_____

Investigation 5

How can iron be separated from cereal?

Enduring Knowledge
Magnets can separate iron from other substances.

Process Skills
communicating, inferring, observing, predicting

Fast Facts
Meteorites are often made of iron and nickel. If a magnet is pulled through dirt, about 20% of the particles that are picked up will be from outer space.

Vocabulary
separate

Materials for Getting Ready
- 1 piece of white paper
- box of iron-fortified cereal
- magnet
- magnifying glass
- newspaper
- shallow pan of dry sand or mixture of sugar and iron filings
- small plastic bag (sandwich size)

Getting Ready
Show students a box of iron-fortified cereal. Ask them if they believe this iron is the same iron found in nails. Have students brainstorm ways to find out whether the iron in the cereal is like the iron in nails. Guide students toward the idea that the iron should be separated from the rest of the cereal and tested with a magnet.

Demonstrate the following technique for separating iron from a substance. Prior to the demonstration, cover a flat surface with newspaper. Fill a shallow pan with sand or a mixture of sugar and iron filings. Place a magnet in a small plastic bag. (The bag will make removing the iron filings from the magnet easy.) Pull the bagged magnet through the sand for several minutes. Hold the bagged magnet over a sheet of white paper and carefully remove the magnet from the bag. Small iron filings should fall onto the paper. Use a magnifying glass to observe the iron filings more closely. Lastly, hold the magnet under the paper to show that the filings are still attracted to it.

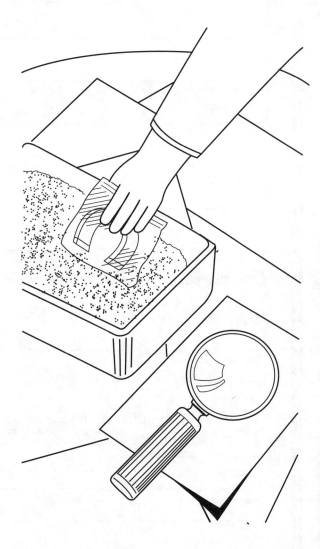

Investigation 5

Materials for Each Group
- 1 piece of white paper
- 2 bowls
- 2 cups of iron-fortified cereal
- Discovery Journals
- magnet
- magnifying glasses
- newspaper for covering desks
- pencils
- small, resealable plastic bag
- spoons
- very warm water

Reflection and Analysis
Allow students to share ways iron was separated from the cereal. Use the questions for a class discussion.

Guiding Questions:
- Which separation method was the most successful? Explain.
- Do you think the iron in cereal is the same iron that is found in nails? How do you know?
- How would you demonstrate that some cereals contain more iron than others?

Guided Exploration
Group students into cooperative teams. Give each team the task of separating iron from cereal. Have students cover their desks or tables with newspaper. Explain that they should use the materials supplied to discover two ways to separate the iron. Instruct students to record their ideas and results in their Discovery Journals.

Encourage students to brainstorm and then test their own ideas. Students may crush the cereal and pass the magnets through the crushed substances. An effective way to separate the iron is to pour very warm water into the cereal and use the magnets (enclosed in plastic bags) to stir the water into the cereal. As the cereal becomes more soggy, iron will separate and will be attracted to the magnet. Have students hold the magnets over pieces of white paper and remove the magnets from the plastic bags.

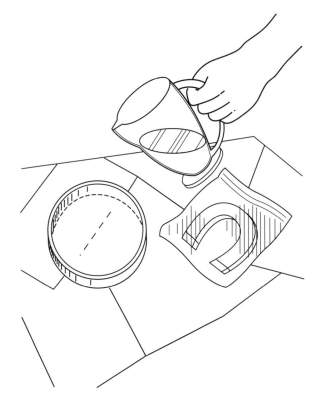

© Carson-Dellosa 17 *Inquiry Investigations: Magnets*

Investigation 6

Do magnets only attract?

Enduring Knowledge
Magnets can attract or repel other magnets.

Process Skills
communicating, observing

Fast Facts
If you break a magnet in half, each half becomes a new magnet. The two magnets will attract and repel like the original magnet.

Vocabulary
attract/attraction, repel/repulsion

Getting Ready
Have students share what they have learned about how magnets interact with other materials. After students share responses, share that you have noticed that magnets attract some, but not all, materials. Pose the question, "Does a magnet only attract?" Ask students is they have ever wanted to eat food that looked good to them, food that they were "attracted to." Ask students if after eating small bites, they found the foods disgusting or delicious. If students did not like the food, ask if they went back for more. Explain to students that magnets, like people, are repulsed by and try to stay away from certain things.

Materials for Each Student
- 2 magnets
- Discovery Journal
- pencil

Guided Exploration
Explain to students that their task is to see how magnets interact with each other. Encourage them to find out if magnets like, or attract, other magnets. If the magnets are not attracted to each other, students should observe what magnets do instead. Explain that as students work they should record their observations in their Discovery Journals.

Reflection and Analysis
Have students share their observations and use the following questions to encourage deeper thinking. After the discussion, have students answer the last question in their journals (page J7) based on their collective experiences.

Guiding Questions:
- What surprised you most about this investigation?
- Did the magnets always attract each other?
- If not, how did they react to each other?
- How do you know how the magnets reacted to each other?

Investigation 7

What is special about the ends of bar magnets?

Enduring Knowledge
The ends of a magnet are called poles. The magnetic pull at the poles is stronger than at the center of the magnet. Like poles repel each other; opposite poles attract each other.

Process Skills
communicating, inferring, observing

Fast Facts
Earth is a giant magnet. Scientists theorize that Earth's magnetic field is due to an electric current generated within Earth's core. This current is created by the flow of the thick liquid outer core around the solid iron-nickel inner core.

Vocabulary
north pole, south pole

Materials for Getting Ready
- bar magnet
- compass
- globe
- marker
- paper
- scissors
- tape

Getting Ready
Explain to students that the ends of magnets have special names—the north pole and the south pole. Set a compass on a flat surface so that students can view it. Place a bar magnet near the compass with an end pointing towards north on the compass. If the compass needle points north, the end of the magnet near the needle is the south pole. If the compass needle points south, the end of the magnet near the needle is the north pole. Identify and label the poles with tape and a marker.

Tape rectangular pieces of paper to the globe to demonstrate a bar magnet passing through Earth. Point out the geographic north and south poles. Ask students to imagine a huge bar magnet passing through Earth. Explain that the ends of the bar would not come out at the geographic north and south poles. One end of the bar would be located in northern Canada, near Ellef Ringnes Island, which is 870 miles (1,400 km) from the geographical north pole. This end of the magnet is the north pole of the magnet and Earth's magnetic north pole. The other end of the bar magnet would come out of the globe off the coast of Wilkes Land, Antarctica, approximately 1,700 miles (2,736 km) from the geographical south pole. This end of the magnet is called the south pole and is the Earth's magnetic south pole.

Materials for Each Student
- 2 bar magnets
- compass
- Discovery Journal
- masking tape
- pencil

Guided Exploration
Have students repeat the procedure to identify the poles of magnets with the help of compasses. Allow time for students to explore the attraction and repulsion characteristics of their magnets. Explain that they should use the questions in their Discovery Journals as guides for placing the poles of the magnets together.

Reflection and Analysis
Have students share their findings and write a rule about the attraction and repulsion properties of magnets using the terms north and south poles. Allow time for students to do the same exploration with different shaped magnets.

Investigation 8
What is a magnetic field?

Enduring Knowledge
A magnet has a force of energy around it called a magnetic field.

Process Skills
communicating, inferring, observing, predicting

Fast Facts
A magnetic field surrounds a magnet in all directions. This field is a three-dimensional force.

Vocabulary
energy, force, magnetic field

Materials for Getting Ready
- 4–5 doughnut-shaped magnets
- pencil or dowel that fits through the center of the magnets

Getting Ready
Review the experiences in Investigation 6 (page 18) in which each student used two magnets to feel the forces of attraction and repulsion. Explain that the pushing and pulling feeling is the energy of magnetism. Share that the amount of magnetic energy is different around the magnet. Ask students, "Where was the attraction and repulsion stronger—at the poles or the sides of the bar magnets? Where was the attraction and repulsion weaker?" Encourage students to draw in their Discovery Journals what they think the shape of the force around the bar magnet looks like. Have students color this area, called the magnetic field, yellow.

Hold a pencil or dowel perpendicular to a flat surface. Place one doughnut-shaped magnet on the pencil. Place a second magnet on the pencil with the same pole facing the first magnet. (The magnets will repel each other. This results in the second magnet hovering above the first.) Add a third magnet, again with the same pole facing the second magnet. Once more, the magnetic forces push against each other causing the third magnet to hover above the second. As you add more magnets to the floating tower, the weight and force increases on the lowest magnets. Because of the larger force and weight, the open spaces between the first, second, and subsequent magnets get smaller.

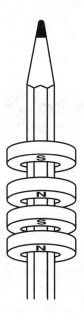

Use the questions to lead a class discussion about the science behind the demonstration:
- Are the magnets really floating? Explain.
- What causes the magnets to hover?
- Why is there more space between three magnets than four?
- What will happen if I remove the pencil?

Investigation 8

Then, have a volunteer draw the floating magnets and label the poles of each magnet on chart paper, an overhead transparency, or the chalkboard.

Materials for Each Student
- 2 bar magnets
- 2 Tbsp. (30 ml) iron filings or finely cut steel wool
- clear plastic such as an overhead transparency
- container with shaker top for iron filings
- Discovery Journal
- pencil
- safety goggles

Guided Exploration

Explain to students that they will be able to see the magnetic field, the force or energy surrounding a magnet, by using iron filings. Model and discuss the following procedures with students prior to their exploration. Explain that students should keep iron filings away from their eyes for safety. Put on safety goggles. Then, place a bar magnet on a flat surface and cover the magnet with clear plastic. Put the iron filings into the container with the shaker top. Next, carefully sprinkle the filings from the container onto the plastic over the area of the magnet. Observe the pattern the filings make. After observing the pattern of the iron filings, open the container with the shaker top. Lift the plastic sheet off the magnet, roll slightly, and slide filings back into their container. After students complete the above procedure, tell them to answer questions 1-3 (page J9). For Discovery Journal questions 4 and 5, have each student use the same procedure with two magnets. Explain that students should place one magnet near, but not touching, the other magnet (for example, pole to pole, side to pole, etc.) and record their results. If time allows, have students repeat the procedure using magnets that are shaped differently.

Reflection and Analysis

Have students share answers to the guiding questions. Students will have discovered that when unlike poles faced each other, the gap between the magnets was filled with iron filings. This is what the magnetic field looks like during attraction. When magnets are placed to repel each other, a gap of iron filings is visible between the two like poles.

Guiding Questions:
- What does the magnetic field look like when north and south poles are near each other?
- What does that tell you about the strength of the magnetism in that area?
- What does the magnetic field look like when two like poles are near each other?
- What does that tell you about the magnetic field between the two magnets?
- Do you think there is magnetic energy above or below the magnets?
- What might the magnetic field of a disk magnet look like? A horseshoe magnet? A doughnut-shaped magnet? How could you find out?
- What could you learn about magnetic fields if you held a magnet near a covered petri dish filled with iron filings?

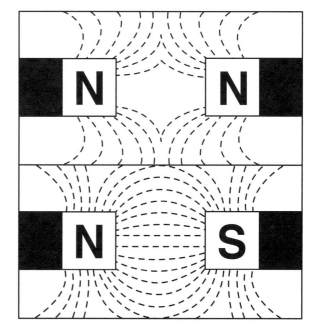

© Carson-Dellosa   CD-2362 *Inquiry Investigations: Magnets*

Investigation 9

Can magnetism travel through other objects?

Enduring Knowledge
A magnetic field can pass through materials that are not made of iron or steel.

Process Skills
classifying, communicating, inferring, observing, predicting

Fast Facts
The magnetic field of energy will pass through any nonmagnetic material without weakening. Place a paper clip in the palm of your hand. Hold a powerful magnet against the back of the same hand and move the paper clip. Amazing!

Vocabulary
magnetization, temporary

Materials for Getting Ready
- 12 in. (30 cm) piece of clear fishing line
- bar magnet
- clear tape
- cloth
- paper clip
- rubber band
- thread

Getting Ready
Tape a bar magnet to the end of a ruler. Cover that end with cloth and secure with a rubber band. Use this ruler as a "magic wand." Tie thread to a paper clip. Tape the loose end of the thread to a flat surface.

Gather students to watch the demonstration. Announce to your class that to begin this investigation you will share some "magic." Create an intriguing story about your magical powers and your ability to wake the "sleeping" paper clip. Wave the "magic wand" over the paper clip. (The paper clip will be attracted to the magnet and rise from the surface toward the wand. The thread prevents the paper clip from attaching to the magnet.)

Ask students to explain what really happened. After listening to students' responses, explain that the magnetic energy passed through the cloth. The paper clip was attracted to the magnet as if the cloth was not there. Invite students to think of ways to determine if magnetic energy passes through other objects.

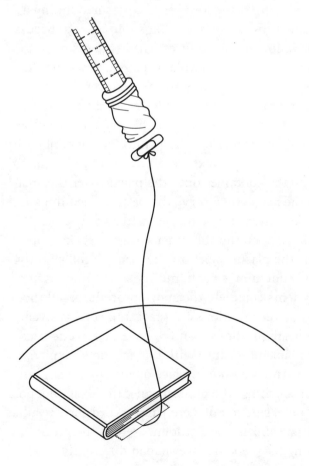

Investigation 9

Materials for Each Group
- bar magnet for each student
- cloth
- cardboard
- coins
- craft sticks
- cups of water
- fabric
- Discovery Journals
- masking tape
- metal jar lids
- metal spoons
- paper (newspaper, construction, copier)
- paper clips
- plastic blocks
- plastic lids
- thread
- wooden rulers or wooden paint stirrers

Reflection and Analysis
In this investigation, students begin to appreciate the "magic" of magnetism. Many students will come to understand that objects made of iron or steel block the magnetic field. Give students the opportunity to share their discoveries and answers to the questions in their Discovery Journals. Then, discuss the guiding questions with the class.

Guiding Questions:
- What items allowed the magnetic field to pass through them?
- Do you think magnetic energy will pass through a thick object? Why or why not?
- Try it. What happened?
- What if two bar magnets were stacked together? How would that change the magnetic field?

Guided Exploration
Using the materials list for suggestions, prepare a bin or basket with items for each group. Explain that students will use their ideas to test the given materials to see if they allow magnetic energy to pass through them. Some students may want to make "magic wands" to repeat your demonstration. Other students may use the ideas generated earlier in the session to test other objects. Explain that students will draw pictures of their testing setups and record observations in their Discovery Journals. Encourage students to share ideas and discoveries.

Home Investigation
This Home Investigation gives students opportunities to teach others at home. Have students make wands at school or send the needed materials for the "magic wands" home. Have each student perform the dancing paper clip trick for someone at home and then reveal the secret behind the "magic." After learning about magnetism, each audience member should complete the homework page by listing three things he learned and answering a question. Explain to students that they should return the completed homework and the "magic wands" to school.

Home Investigation

Name: _____ Date: _____

Investigation 9: Can magnetism travel through other objects?

Magnet Magic

A great secret has been revealed to you—the secret of magnetism. Your skilled teacher has given you knowledge you must share. Please list three things you have learned from your teacher about the secret of magnetism.

1. _____
_____
_____

2. _____
_____
_____

3. _____
_____
_____

After learning these things, do you think magnetism can travel through other objects? Why or why not?

_____
_____
_____
_____
_____

Investigation 10

How strong is my magnet?

Enduring Knowledge
Magnets have different strengths.

Process Skills
communicating, inferring, measuring, observing, predicting

Fast Facts
A magnet's force is greater than Earth's gravity. A magnet defies gravity by easily sticking to the side of a refrigerator. A magnet is strongest at the poles. The centers of magnets have almost no magnetism.

Vocabulary
magnetization

Materials for Getting Ready
- 2 powerful bar magnets
- 2 powerful horseshoe magnets
- 20 or more paper clips

Getting Ready
Have two students face each other and hold horseshoe magnets. Ask students to hold the magnets so that the opposite poles attract each other. After students separate the magnets, ask how strong they think the horseshoe magnets are. Next, have them try the same task with two bar magnets. Ask students what they think about the strength of the bar magnets. Ask the class how they were able to predict the strength of the magnets.

Ask students how they describe their own physical strength. A student might say something like, "I can lift my little sister, who weighs thirty pounds." Pose the questions, "Could we measure the strength of a magnet by measuring how much of something the magnet can lift? What could we use to discover the strength of a magnet?"

Have students brainstorm ideas. Explain that they will use paper clips to test the strength of a bar magnet. Use a horseshoe magnet to model this measuring procedure. Place a paper clip on the side of a horseshoe magnet near a pole. Tell students that this paper clip becomes a temporary magnet and this phenomenon is called magnetization. Attach one paper clip to the first paper clip. Add paper clips until the chain drops or breaks.

Materials for Each Student
- 20 or more paper clips (depending on magnets' strength)
- bar magnet
- Discovery Journal
- horseshoe, disc shaped, or other types of magnets
- pencil

Guided Exploration
Have students use their Discovery Journals as guides for where to place the first paper clips on their magnets. Students will test strength at different areas of the magnet to determine if magnets have strong spots. Students also need time to experiment with different types of magnets and methods for exploring magnet strength.

Reflection and Analysis
As a class, determine which type of magnet is strongest and weakest. Then, discuss the questions.

Guiding Questions:
- Do the magnetic field drawings (page J9) give you ideas about where a magnet is strongest?
- How does the magnetic strength of the bar magnet compare to the horseshoe magnet?
- How do the size and shape of a magnet affect its magnetic strength?
- What other ways did you try to measure magnetic strength? Which way was better or not as good?
- If you put two magnets together, do you think they will be twice as strong?

Investigation 11

How can I make my own magnet?

Enduring Knowledge
A magnet can be used to make an item made of iron or steel into a temporary magnet.

Process Skills
communicating, inferring, measuring, observing, predicting

Fast Facts
Stroking objects of iron or steel with magnets can magnetize those objects. Iron is a weaker metal that magnetizes easily, but will not stay magnetized long. Steel is a metal that is more difficult to magnetize, but will become a stronger, longer lasting magnet. Permanent magnets are often made of steel.

Vocabulary
atom, permanent, stroke, temporary

Getting Ready
Read aloud *Mickey's Magnet* by Franklyn M. Branley and Eleanor K. Vaughan (1976). In this story, Mickey learns how to make his own magnet. Your students can, too. Based on what they heard in the story, ask students to name the supplies they will need to make their own magnets. The story mentions a magnet, needle, and pins. Staples are recommended instead of pins because they are lighter and therefore more likely to be attracted to a needle-magnet. Supply students with materials and have them make their own magnets.

Materials for Each Student
- 3-4 in. (7.6-10.2 cm) common nails (iron)
- bar magnet
- Discovery Journal
- large steel needle (with point dulled by a file)
- pencil
- individual staples

Guided Exploration
Explain that to make a magnet, a student should hold the eye end of the needle in one hand and stroke the needle with a pole end of a magnet. Tell each student to always stroke in one direction, being certain to lift the magnet at the point of the needle, place it back down near the eye, stroke to the point, lift, and repeat. A needle will require 20 or more strokes to become magnetized. Next, challenge students to magnetize iron nails. Have students refer to the Discovery Journals for the procedure and questions.

Reflection and Analysis
Have students discuss their experiences with making their own magnets. Ask why they think it was necessary to stroke the needles and nails in only one direction. Explain the structure of a magnet as described in the following paragraphs. Create an overhead transparency of the illustration on page 27.

If a magnet is broken in half, each half will be a functional magnet. If those magnets are broken in half, each piece will continue to function as a magnet. Continue to imagine breaking each piece of magnet in half, smaller and smaller, until you have the smallest bit of magnet. It would be too small to view without a very powerful microscope. That smallest piece of magnet is called an atom.

Investigation 11

An atom is a scientific word for the tiniest bit of something. Each atom is a magnet with a north and a south pole. In a piece of non-magnetized iron or steel, the atoms are arranged randomly (See illustration at top right.) In a magnet, however, the north poles of the atoms all face the same direction. (See illustration at bottom right.) This arrangement of atoms is what gives the iron or steel magnetism—all of the energy from the lined up atoms works to create a magnet.

Explain to students that their magnets are temporary magnets, meaning that the magnetic energy in them will not last long. Tell students that permanent magnets are like the bar and horseshoe magnets. They are made of stronger metals, such as steel, and are magnetized with electricity. Permanent magnets, when well cared for, can last a long time.

On the back of page J12 in the Discovery Journal, have each student draw a picture of what she thinks the arrangement of atoms looked like before she magnetized the needle and label the picture "needle not magnetized."

Next, have each student draw a picture of what he thinks the arrangement of atoms looked like after he magnetized the needle and label the picture "magnet."

Discuss the following questions.

Guiding Questions:
- What happened to the atoms when you stroked the needle?
- Why was it important to stroke the needle or nail in only one direction?
- What do you suppose would happen to the atoms if you rubbed the needle back and forth with the magnet?

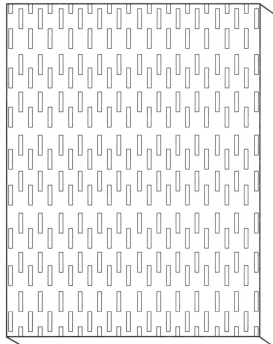

Investigation 12

How can I demagnetize a magnet?

Enduring Knowledge
A magnet can lose its energy when rubbed back and forth with another magnet, dropped, hit, or exposed to high temperatures over time.

Process Skills
communicating, inferring, measuring, observing, predicting

Fast Facts
To increase the life of permanent magnets, store them side by side with the opposite poles near each other. Place a "keeper," or iron bar, across the ends of a horseshoe magnet.

Vocabulary
demagnetize

Materials for Getting Ready
- candle
- cool water (to fill bowl)
- common nail
- matches
- paper clips
- small bowl
- tongs

Getting Ready
Silence builds a sense of interest, so begin the demonstration without speaking while magnetizing a nail. Test the nail with paper clips and then light a candle. Hold the nail with tongs and put the end of the nail into the flame for one minute. Dip the nail into cool water. Test the magnetism with paper clips. If the nail still picks up paper clips, repeat the procedure. Hold the nail in the flame for two to three minutes and test again.

Ask students to describe what happened during the demonstration. Have them share what happened to the atoms when they were heated by the candle. Guide students to understand that the heat caused the atoms to move, and in turn, moved them out of alignment into a random arrangement. The heat caused the magnet to demagnetize.

Materials for Each Student
- bar magnet
- Discovery Journal
- paper clips
- pencil
- two 3-4 in. (7.6-10.2 cm) common nails (iron)

Guided Exploration
Challenge students to find ways to demagnetize magnets. Have each student magnetize two nails, brainstorm ways to alter the alignment of the atoms, and ultimately demagnetize the nails. Explain that students should complete the charts in their Discovery Journals as they experiment. Encourage students to share ideas and guide them when needed. They may need support to think of other things besides heat that will successfully demagnetize the nails. Nails lose their magnetism after about ten minutes. Dropping a nail many times or stroking a nail with a magnet in the opposite direction or with a back-and-forth motion will also demagnetize the nail.

Reflection and Analysis
Explain that permanent magnets require care because they, like temporary magnets, can lose their magnetic strength. Have students brainstorm ways to care for magnets. Teach students the proper way to store magnets; then discuss the questions.
- Which method of demagnetization was most successful? Why?
- Why do materials lose their magnetic strength?

Investigation 13

What is an electromagnet?

Enduring Knowledge
An electromagnet is a temporary magnet. Electricity is used to control magnetism by turning it on or off.

Process Skills
communicating, inferring, measuring, observing, predicting

Fast Facts
Permanent magnets are made using electricity. Metal detectors and maglev trains are electromagnets.

Vocabulary
circuit, electromagnet, negative, positive

Getting Ready
Explain to students that whereever there is electricity there are electromagnetic fields. Wire carrying electricity has a magnetic field around it. Electro means electricity, so an electromagnet is a magnet created by electricity. Have students brainstorm ways an electromagnet could be created by electricity.

Draw a basic electric circuit on the board or overhead projector. Explain that a battery is a source of electricity. If one end of a wire is attached to one side of a battery and the other end is attached to the other side of the battery, electricity flows from the battery through the wire and back to the battery. A circle of electricity is created. This circle of electricity is called a circuit.

The electricity flowing through the wire can be used to light a lightbulb, turn on a TV, or run other electrical devices. This moving electricity can also be used to make an electromagnet.

Materials for Each Student
- 2 D-cell non-alkaline batteries
- 3-4 in. (7.6-10.2 cm) common nail (iron)
- about 47 in. (119.4 cm) of insulated copper (bell) wire
- Discovery Journal
- electrical tape
- paper clips
- pencil
* wire cutters

Guided Exploration
Guide students in making electromagnets. (See illustration on J14.) Cut insulated copper wire into pieces about 47 in. (119 cm) long. Strip 1 in. (2.5 cm) of insulation off each end of wire. Tape two D-cell non-alkaline batteries together with electrical tape. Be sure the positive pole of one battery is touching the negative pole of the other. Wrap the wire in a neat coil around a nail. Leave about a 6 in. (15 cm) length of wire loose at each end of the nail. Use electrical tape to secure one end of the bare wire to one battery pole. Tape the other end of the wire to the other battery pole. If everything is attached correctly, the nail will be magnetic. Test how many paper clips are attracted to the nail. Loosen the wire from one end of the battery and watch the paper clips drop. Give students opportunities to test their electromagnets on different items. **After completing this exploration, have each student disconnect one end of the wire for the next investigation.**

Reflection and Analysis
Have students discuss the questions.

Guiding Questions:
- Why should the wire touch both poles?
- Where else can you find electromagnets?

Investigation 14

How does electromagnetic strength change?

Enduring Knowledge
The strength of an electromagnet depends on the number of coils of wire around the nail and the amount of current flowing through the wire. The more times the wire is wrapped around the nail, the stronger the electromagnet becomes. An electromagnet becomes stronger when more electricity flows through the wire.

Process Skills
communicating, inferring, measuring, observing, predicting

Fast Facts
Very strong electromagnets are used in shipping yards. The electromagnets lift large metallic storage trailers off the decks of cargo ships and transport the trailers to waiting trains or trucks.

Vocabulary
coil

Getting Ready
Ask students to imagine how an electromagnet might be useful in a junkyard. After listening to students' responses, explain that in order to separate metal, an electromagnet is attached to a crane. The crane lowers the large magnet into a pile of junk. An electromagnet is turned on and pieces of iron and steel are attracted to the magnet. The crane lifts the electromagnet with the metal attached and moves the metal to a waiting dump truck to be recycled. When the electromagnet is turned off, the metal falls into the bed of the truck.

Materials for Each Pair
- 2 D-cell non-alkaline batteries
- electrical tape
- electromagnets from Investigation 13
- Discovery Journals
- paper clips
- pencils

Guided Exploration
As a class, brainstorm ways to change the strength of an electromagnet. Tell students that they will work in pairs and use their electromagnets from Investigation 13. Explain that as students make changes to the electromagnets they need to record that information in their Discovery Journals. Remind them that the more paper clips it attracts, the stronger an electromagnet is. If students need guidance, suggest increasing the number of batteries in the circuit or coils around the nail.

Reflection and Analysis
Have students share their observations. Ask the following questions to reinforce that adding more electricity or more coils of wire will strengthen electromagnets.

Guiding Questions:
- What types of changes did you make to your electromagnets that were successful?
- How do you know they were successful?
- What changes did not work? Why did they not work?
- What are the two things you can do to increase an electromagnet's strength?

© Carson-Dellosa   CD-2362 *Inquiry Investigations: Magnets*

Investigation 15

How can I use magnets for fun?

Enduring Knowledge
Creating and inventing are important parts of being a scientist.

Process Skills
communicating

Fast Facts
Magnets are used in many places for many things including motors (refrigerator, air conditioner, furnace, etc.), computers, generators, power plants, subways, trains, radar systems, nuclear energy research, medical diagnosis, audiotapes, videotapes, and toys.

Vocabulary
invention

Getting Ready
This investigation ends with Magnet Fun Day. On this day students will share games or activities they made using magnets. This investigation's concept is simple—using one's prior knowledge and imagination to make something new is part of being a scientist. Students can complete their inventions at school or at home. To help inspire students, read excerpts from the suggested books (page 7).

Materials for the Class
- bar magnets
- books about inventions
- boxes (assorted sizes and types)
- colored pencils
- construction paper
- glue
- markers
- masking tape

Materials for the Class Contd.
- pencils
- rulers
- recyclables (egg cartons, paper tubes, plastic lids, etc.)
- scissors

Guided Exploration
If this investigation is used for homework, introduce the project in class and have students complete the Discovery Journal pages at home. Be sure to send home magnets, as well.

If students complete this investigation at school, gather materials in advance. Encourage students to bring recyclable items from home. Give students ample time to create and develop ideas, to make the projects, and to make changes. Have students name their projects and write instructions to accompany their inventions. Set aside a date for Magnet Fun Day and allow students to share their projects.

Reflection and Analysis
After students have given their presentations, discuss the following questions. Invite other classes to try out the activities. Then, have students answer the questions in their Discovery Journals (page J16).

Guiding Questions:
- If you had more time or different materials, what would you do differently?
- How did classmates use magnets in new and interesting ways?

Home Investigation
Use the Home Investigation worksheet (page 32) if students are doing their projects at home. Before sending it home, fill in the date for Magnet Fun Day and read the reproducible aloud.

Home Investigation

Name: _____ Date: _____

Investigation 15: How can I use magnets for fun?

Magnet Fun Day is coming soon. On _____, we will be sharing games or activities that you created using magnets. Use the blank space for notes and drawings.

1. Make up a game, activity, or product that uses magnets in some way. Use things from home, but make sure to ask a grown-up what materials you may use for your project.

2. Next, think of a name for your project. Create a sign with the name of your project and your name.

3. Last, write rules for your game or activity or instructions for how to use what you made. Tell how many people can use your product or play your game, and how to use what you made or how to play the game. Write a rough draft first and have someone look over it. Then, write a neat copy or use a computer for a final copy.

_____
_____
_____
_____
_____

Discovery Journal

Date:_____

Investigation 1: What are magnets?

1. List what you know about magnets.
   _____
   _____

2. Describe your magnet. What does it look like? What do you think it is made of?
   _____
   _____

3. List the things your magnet attracts.
   _____
   _____

4. List the things your magnet does not attract.
   _____
   _____

5. What did you discover about the things the magnet attracts?
   _____
   _____

6. What did you discover about the things the magnet does not attract?
   _____
   _____

7. Based on your observations, what are magnets?
   _____
   _____

Discovery Journal

Date:_____

Investigation 2: How can magnets help me find hidden objects?

Be a Magnet Detective! Use your magnet to find the location of each hidden object. After your teacher reveals each object, write the name of the object next to the correct number.

Item	Location
1.	
2.	
3.	
4.	
5.	
6.	
7.	
8.	
9.	
10.	

How did the magnet help you find the hidden objects?

_____
_____
_____
_____

Discovery Journal

Date:_____

Investigation 3: What materials are attracted to magnets?

Look at the items in your bag. First, write down the name of each item and from what material it is made. Make a prediction about each item's attraction to magnets. Then, use the magnet to test your predictions. Record your results.

Item	Material	Prediction (Yes or No)	Results (Yes or No)
1.			
2.			
3.			
4.			
5.			
6.			

1. Did any results surprise you? If so, why?

_____

_____

_____

2. Were all of the metal items attracted to the magnet? Why or why not?

_____

_____

_____

_____

Discovery Journal

Date:_____

Investigation 4: What metals are attracted to magnets?

Write the name of each item and the material from which it is made. If you do not know what type of metal was used to make the item, look on the chart on the next page. Test each item and record the results.

Item	Metal	Results (Yes or No)
1.		
2.		
3.		
4.		
5.		
6.		
7.		
8.		

1. Which metals are attracted to the magnet?
   _____
   _____

2. Write a rule about what magnets attract.
   _____
   _____
   _____

Discovery Journal

Date:_____

Investigation 4: What metals are attracted to magnets?

The chart below shows products made out of metal. Use this information to help you figure out what type of metals make up the items you are testing for magnetism.

Product	Type of Metal
jewelry	silver or gold
nail	iron
wire	copper
straight pin	steel or brass coated with silver
screw	iron or brass
aluminum foil	aluminum
penny	bronze
nickel	copper and nickel
dime	copper middle and copper and nickel outer layer
quarter	copper middle and copper and nickel outer layer
dollar coin	copper middle and alloy material
spoon	stainless steel or silver
can	steel
paper clip	steel or brass
steel wool	steel
pewter bowl	tin

Discovery Journal

Date: _____

Investigation 5: How can iron be separated from cereal?

With your team, review the supplies you have been given. Together, think of two ways you can try to separate iron from cereal.

1. Write about your first idea. Draw how the filings looked when you tried the idea.
   _____
   _____

2. Write about your second idea. Draw how the filings looked when you tried the idea.
   _____
   _____

Discovery Journal

Date:_____

Investigation 6: Do magnets only attract?

1. Hold two magnets near each other in different positions and describe what happens.

   _____
   _____
   _____
   _____
   _____
   _____
   _____

2. Does a magnet only attract? Explain.

   _____
   _____
   _____
   _____
   _____
   _____
   _____

3. A magnet can attract another magnet. A magnet can also repel another magnet. What does the word **repel** mean?

   _____
   _____
   _____
   _____
   _____

Discovery Journal

Date:_____

Investigation 7: What is special about the ends of bar magnets?

After the north and south poles of your bar magnets are labeled with masking tape, use the magnets to answer the questions.

1. What happens when you touch the north pole of one magnet to the south pole of the other magnet?
   _____
   _____

2. What happens when you touch the north poles of both magnets together?
   _____
   _____

3. What happens when you touch the south poles of both magnets together?
   _____
   _____

4. Continue to touch a pole of one magnet to different areas of the other magnet. What do you notice happening?
   _____
   _____
   _____
   _____

5. What rule could you write about the way the poles of magnets attract or repel?
   _____
   _____
   _____

Discovery Journal

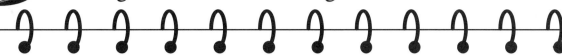

Date:_____

Investigation 8: What is a magnetic field?

1. Draw what you think the shape of the force of magnetic energy around a bar magnet looks like. Color this area yellow.

2. After completing the investigation, draw what you think the magnetic field looks like.

3. Where do you think the magnet is the strongest? Why?

_____

4. Does the magnetic field change when two magnets are placed near each other? Try to find out and draw the results.

Like Poles	Unlike Poles	Side to Side

© Carson-Dellosa   CD-2362 *Inquiry Investigations: Magnets*

Discovery Journal

Date:_____

Investigation 9: Can magnetism travel through other objects?

Test different materials to see if a magnet's energy will pass through each material and attract a paper clip. Think of a way to set up your materials to complete the testing.

1. Draw a picture of your setup and label the parts.

2. Complete the chart for each object you test.

Item	Material	Prediction	Results
A.			
B.			
C.			
D.			

3. Circle the items in the chart that allow the magnetic field to pass through them.

4. Write a rule about magnetism passing through objects.

_____

_____

5. Do you think magnetic energy will pass through a thick object? Why or why not? Try it.

_____

_____

Discovery Journal

Date:_____

Investigation 10: How strong is my magnet?

Measure how strong your magnet is by adding paper clips to your magnet to make a paper clip chain. When the clips fall or the chain breaks, count how many paper clips your magnet could hold in that area and record the answer. The chart below tells you where to place the first paper clip for each chain.

Location of First Paper Clip	Number of Paper Clips
side edge closest to the north pole	
north pole	
side edge closest to the south pole	
south pole	
middle of magnet	

1. Is one part of the magnet stronger than another? Explain.
   _____
   _____

2. Do you think that all kinds of magnets have certain parts that are stronger than other parts? Explain.
   _____
   _____

3. How could you find out if all magnets have the same strong area?
   _____
   _____

4. Write a rule about the strongest areas on magnets.
   _____

Discovery Journal

Date:_____

Investigation 11: How can I make my own magnet?

Test the needle or nail to make sure it is not already magnetized. Make your own magnets.

1. What do you have to do to magnetize the needle or nail?
   _____

2. What direction do you have to stroke the needle or nail in?
   _____

3. Stroke the needle the number of times listed on the chart. Test your new "magnet" by picking up staples. Record the results.

Number of Total Strokes	Number of Staples Picked Up
10	
20	
30	
40	

4. What happened to the strength of the needle the more it was stroked?
   _____

5. If you stroke a nail with a magnet, will it be stronger or weaker than the needle? Why?
   _____
   _____

6. Compare the strength of the magnetized nail to the strength of the magnetized needle.
   _____
   _____

Discovery Journal

Date:_____

Investigation 12: How can I demagnetize a magnet?

Magnetize a nail by stroking it with a magnet. Remember to stroke the nail in only one direction. Test the magnet's strength and record the number of paper clips held by the nail in the following chart. Try to demagnetize the nail. Record what you tried. Test the nail again and record how many paper clips it held.

Nail Strength Before Change	Change Made	After Change Nail Strength	(Yes or No) Demagnetized

1. Draw a picture of what the atoms look like in a demagnetized nail.

2. How can you handle magnets so that they stay magnetized?

_____
_____
_____
_____
_____

Discovery Journal

Date:_____

Investigation 13: What is an electromagnet?

Cut insulated copper wire into pieces about 47 in. (119 cm) long. Strip 1 in. (2.5 cm) of insulation off each end of wire. Tape two D-cell non-alkaline batteries together with electrical tape. Be sure the positive pole of one battery is touching the negative pole of the other. Wrap the wire in a neat coil around a nail. Leave about a 6 in. (15 cm) length loose at each end of the nail. Use electrical tape to secure one end of the bare wire to one battery pole. Tape the other end of the wire to the other battery pole.

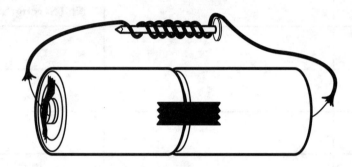

1. How many paper clips does the electromagnet hold?
   _____

2. Disconnect one wire. What happens to the paper clips?
   _____
   _____

3. What is special about an electromagnet?
   _____
   _____
   _____
   _____

4. When would an electromagnet be useful?
   _____
   _____

Discovery Journal

Date:_____

Investigation 14: How does electromagnetic strength change?

First, test your electromagnet to see how many paper clips it attracts. Remember to make only one change at a time, record the change, and then test the electromagnet to see if it picks up more paper clips. Repeat the procedure three more times.

State of Electromagnet	Number of Paper Clips
Original electromagnet—no changes	
Change 1	
Change 2	
Change 3	
Change 4	

1. Which was the strongest electromagnet you made?
   _____

2. Why do you think this change worked?
   _____
   _____
   _____

3. What change did not work and why?
   _____
   _____
   _____
   _____

Discovery Journal

Date: _____

Investigation 15: How can I use magnets for fun?

1. List five things you have learned about magnets and magnetism.
   _____
   _____
   _____
   _____
   _____
   _____
   _____
   _____
   _____
   _____

2. List three things you have learned about creating something new and fun.
   _____
   _____
   _____
   _____
   _____
   _____
   _____
   _____

© Carson-Dellosa — CD-2362 *Inquiry Investigations: Magnets*